Practice Soccer at Home

Chest Dugger

Table Of Contents

ABOUT THE AUTHOR

Chest Dugger is a soccer fan, former professional and coach, looking to share his knowledge. Enjoy this book and several others that he has written.

DISCLAIMER

INTRODUCTION

At times like these, when a global pandemic is threatening lives across all nations, soccer falls into perspective. Actually, we have discovered, it isn't more important than life or death, despite the oft made claims to the contrary.

But the plague will pass, and life will return to a normality of sorts soon enough. While we wait, anxiously, for that moment, it is important to stay fit. As good a way as any is to use our individual fitness regimes to help improve our soccer skills at the same time.

So many coaching books require complex equipment, copious resources and fantastic facilities. In writing 'Practice Soccer at Home', we are seeking to offer a guide for those times when we train alone, in our back yard, with little more than a ball and our immediate environment. Undertaking this additional work is important whether we are professionals seeking to perfect our technique at the highest level (why else would top professionals build home gyms into their luxurious houses?) or, more relevantly for this book, keen amateurs or youth players looking to develop our own game.

With jobs to hold down, school to attend and such like, it is unlikely that, in the best of times, we will get more than two formal training sessions per week, plus a match at the weekend. Realistically, it is likely to be just one session. In order to maximise our potential, we must do some work on our skills and endurance alone. The most practical place for many of us is to undertake this training at home. Why get in the car to drive to the gym or park if we have a back yard we could use instead? The answer is, of course, what to do in the back yard, and what to do it with! This book provides some answers to those questions.

Seeking a small silver lining to even the darkest of clouds, such as the one circulating the world at the time of writing, we can see that for those of us consigned to home, self-isolating or acting on the instructions of our Governments, we do at least have the time to get outside with a ball and hone those skills which have thus far eluded us.

For the tips and drills that follow we have assumed a back yard of 30 metres by 30 metres. We have assumed access to a wall, or some other form of rebound. We will highlight some useful commercial products which can make our practice easier. Nothing too expensive, though. Beyond that we will make suggestions of everyday items we can use to help set up the drills and practices. Where a drill can be made easier to follow with the use of an illustration, we have added a diagram. In total, this book contains:

- Drills for individuals, pairs and small groups to try in their backyard,

- Numerous tips to get the most from a session,
- Some solo, paired and small group games to make training fun,
- Exercises that can be undertaken at home and in the backyard to improve fitness and flexibility,
- Some mental health guidance,
- Outlines of key techniques for reference,
- Key skills on which the drills work,
- More than thirty diagrams to help with understanding the more complex drills.

The key for the diagrams illustrating some of the drills is as follows:

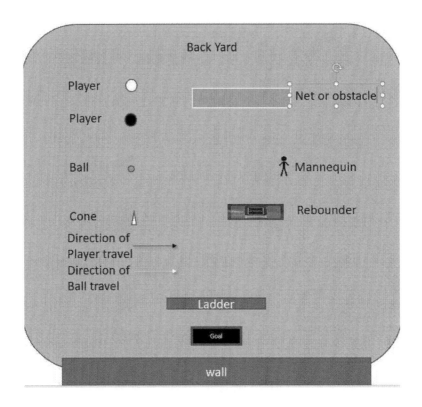

Equipment to Enhance Home Training

As explained in the introduction, we will be assuming that training from home means that we have no specialist soccer equipment at hand. Each of the drills and tips we offer will use everyday items we can substitute for specialist equipment.

Notwithstanding that, when we play the game the substitute is on the bench because he or she is not quite up to scratch to make the starting line-up, for whatever reason. They are a perfectly good stand in when needed. They might even re-energise a team when a part of it is worn out and tired, and in need of substitution themselves.

But if they were good enough to start, then they would not have been warming the bench. The same applies with our make-shift items for drills. They will allow us to work out, to practise our skills and develop our technique. But they are maybe not as good as professionally made equipment. Therefore, in this opening chapter we have identified some accessories that will make it a little easier, and a little more effective to train at home. We have limited each individual purchase to $100, less if at all possible. To help readers around the world, we have offered a ball-park price over which consumers should not look to pay, and offered this not only US dollars, but also Euros, Australian Dollars and Pounds Sterling.

Fitness and Exercise

Number One – Fitness Exercise Equipment : Home Weights

Travel sets of weights are great for use in the home, because they are usually water filled, and therefore can be easily stored when not in use. They can, of course, relatively easily be packed for the annual vacation, and a twenty-minute workout might enable us to justify that extra cocktail or additional scoop of ice-cream.

Travel Dumbbells: Pay around $50

Ankle Weights help to strengthen leg muscles by adding resistance to work outs.

Ankle Weights: Pay no more than $30

Number Two - Tip: Home Made Weights

We can, though, make a perfectly usable set of weights from everyday items. A gallon plastic container filled with water makes a fine object for adding resistance.

We can use it to develop leg muscles by adding resistance to lifts, place it in a ruck sack to make jogging more strenuous or simply lift it as we might a set of standard weights. For more specific work, find a small, 400g can size container with a plastic lid. The chances are that this will not be waterproof and will have been used to hold dried goods originally. However, we can place a plastic bag filled with water, carefully and tightly tied, inside, put the lid back on and use it for curls or similar lifts.

Number Three - Drill Equipment: Cones

A set of cones is a perfect starting point for many of the drills we can practice on our own. They are very inexpensive, and easily stored. The flat cones are perfectly acceptable, although traffic style cones are slightly more flexible, although a lot more expensive.

Cones – fifty flat cones plus holder expect to pay $15

Expect to pay a similar amount for a pack of a dozen traffic style cones. Twelve should be sufficient for most drills in a back yard.

Number Four - Tip: Homemade dribbling cones

We can create our own cones by saving plastic containers. Anything from butter holders, to gravy powder cases to old Tupperware boxes will work well enough. Simply put some soil inside to give a little weight and put the lid on top.

Number Five – Drill Equipment: Other Soccer Aids

Soccer is about scoring goals and pop up soccer goal varieties are surprisingly inexpensive. They might cost a little more than a couple of jumpers, or garden canes stuck into the grass, but it is hard to replicate the thrill of the net bulging backwards with an old pair or towels, or whatever. Here are three examples, each slightly different.

An eight feet by five feet portable goal – expect to pay in the region of from $50. Clearly, the more that is paid, the more robust the goal is likely to be.

For a small, temporary goal which will probably only last a few months, expect to pay in the region of $25.

11

Finally, for a popular pop up goal, expect to pay (depending on quality, which varies hugely in this market) $30 - $120. Note, the lower price is for a pair of small pop up goals.

It is possible to get goals which include target areas. These are really handy for shooting and passing accuracy, especially in a small space like a back yard. Small versions of these, which double up as pop up goals, can be purchased for the following:

$20

After a goal, the next most useful piece of equipment for drills to work on at home is a set of mannequins. These are relatively expensive, but are easily stored, and will add an element of opposition pressure that cannot be achieved if we are practicing alone.

Expect to pay something in the region of $30 for a four-foot-tall spiked example of reasonably good quality, certainly adequate for home use. We particularly liked, though, a set of three spring back mannequins. They do not particularly look like people, but that does not really matter. However, the price represented good value for something that also give the opportunity to work on rebounds.

$85

Other equipment which will prove handy to have at home includes:

Agility ladders, handy for speed work, agility and general fitness. $25

Rebounders – very useful for passing drills and first touch in particular. From $50.

Hoops – great for target practice with passing and shooting. For a pack of five, expect to pay in the region of $18.

Number Six - Tip: Making Our Own Soccer Equipment

We can try to avoid the expense of purchases with a little ingenuity.

Goals – besides the obvious of a couple of jumpers or a pair of thin poles hammered into the ground we could:

- Chalk a goal on a wall or garden fence, steering clear of windows, of course,
- Fill a couple of plastic plant pots with soil and stick the thickest garden canes we can find inside to represent posts. The especially artistically adept can tie a length of twine between the posts, to stretch taut and use as a crossbar marker when the goal is laid out.

Target areas – if we have hoops and a goal, these can be suspended from the cross bar on pieces of string. Or, hung from a cloth line / tree.

We can chalk targets on a wall or fence (provided it is strong enough). We can suspend large butter or margarine containers on pieces of string to represent targets, again hanging them from a line at different heights, or from the cross bar of a garden goal.

Mannequins are a little more challenging. However, by filling a sports bag with old clothes or towels it becomes relatively solid. Stood on its end, it will support a second bag on top, making a moderately sized mannequin to shoot or play around.

Three ideas for creating our own agility ladder:

- Paint it straight onto the grass, or chalk onto a patio or decking,
- Using cones, or butter containers, thread a small length of string between two, stretch out and place on the floor. We need at least 16 containers to make a ladder of reasonable use,
- If we have a footpath made of paving slabs in the back yard, use the cracks between the slabs as the rungs of the ladder, or chalk them on.

For the rebounder, you can use a wall.

Hoops are difficult to recreate, but we can use large storage crates to be targets. These can be turned on their side to make a 'goal' target.

So, with the equipment in place that we need to offer a good variety of home alone drills and practices, we can move on to finding some inventive ways of using our back yards as the new home to replace, or supplement, our standard training sessions.

Home Fitness – Warming Up, Developing Stamina and Building Muscle

We will start with strength and fitness, since these will both quickly fade if we go for a long period without paying them good attention. In these times of self-isolation, different countries, states and regions are placing their own restrictions on where people may go, with whom (if anybody outside the immediate family) they can mix and for how long such restrictions on normal life will apply.

However, whilst these physical exercises and drills are particularly important in times when normal training is impossible, for any reason, they are also very useful drills and exercises to employ alongside a normal weekly, or twice weekly, soccer training session.

Let us start with warming up.

The main muscle groups that soccer players use is in the legs. While unable to play the game competitively for a while, it is important that we keep these muscles in as good a shape as possible. If we are planning on an intensive training session at home, it is also important to make sure that we have properly warmed these up.

It is bad enough being out injured at any time, but during a period when exercise is double, triply important, it is even more essential that we look after our bodies. Warming up and stretching is a vital part of this.

Number Seven - Fitness Exercise: Get the Quads Quivering

Stand approximately one meter from a solid wall. Lean forward and put out our left arm until it touches the wall and is able to support our body weight. Lift the right leg, and bend at the knee. Hold the right foot with the right hand, somewhere around the lower shin or ankle region, and lift slowly and smoothly.

After a few inches we will sense the quad muscles tightening. At this point, hold the pose for ten seconds and slowly relax. Do not 'bounce' the stretched leg, and do not take it so far that pain is caused.

Repeat five times, then work on the other leg.

Number Eight - Fitness Exercise: Comfy Calves

The calf muscle is a particularly vulnerable one for soccer players, because of all the twisting and turning which takes place at speed. Therefore, it is important to give some time to this handy muscle. The following drill is simple, but effective.

Once more, lean against the wall. Either arm is fine for this drill. Place one foot around two feet in front of the other. Bend the knee of the front leg, while straightening the rear leg. We will be able to feel the calf muscle on our rear leg begin to stretch. As before, do not take it to the point of pain, but hold for around ten seconds, relax and repeat four or five times.

Then swap legs to repeat on the other calf.

Number Nine - Fitness Exercise: Hot Hips

This is a very gentle hip exercise but performed daily will help ensure flexibility without placing any significant strain on the joint.

Start by kneeling on the ground. Take one leg and stretch it out in front until the sole of the foot is completely on the floor, as though being on one knee and about to propose. (Thus, making this an especially handy drill for those madly in love.) Gently push through the extended leg, rest for a couple of seconds, and return to the starting position.

Repeat this drill five times, then swap to the other side.

Number Ten - Fitness Exercise: Hearty Hamstrings

When a soccer player 'does a hammy', boy do they know it. The sudden, searing pain that shoots upwards and downwards from the point of the tear. The overwhelming need to straighten the muscle and grip it like holding the hands of a small child crossing a narrow, swaying rope bridge. Anybody who has pulled a hamstring will understand the necessity of dramatic language to describe the pain. Anybody who has not, trust one who has…this is something you do not wish to experience.

Fortunately, stretching a ham string during a warmup is one of the easiest exercises to do. Sit on the floor with the legs stretched in front of us. We reach forward and grab our feet with our hands. In this position, we simply rock forwards and backwards, gently, for thirty seconds. Have a thirty second rest, then repeat. If you seeing your knee bending while you try to reach your feet, you can keep your knees straight and reach a point further away from your feet.

A little warning about the hamstring. If we have suffered a pull, having put too much strain on the muscle after a long period of relative inactivity, exercise will only make it worse (something true of all muscle injuries, but especially so with the hamstring.) Unfortunately, unless we have access to a trained physio, the only action we can take is rest.

Number Eleven- Fitness Exercise: Butterfly Stretch the Groin

For this important, if somewhat ungainly, drill we sit on the floor, point our knees outwards and put the souls of our feet together. Next, we grab our feet, and gently exert pressure to pull them towards us. As with other drills, we stop before pain is felt, but when we feel our

19

muscles stretching, hold for ten seconds, gently relax and repeat four or five times.

Number Twelve - Fitness Exercise: Avoiding an Aching Achilles

A rupture of the Achilles is one of the few non skeletal injuries where the pain exceeds that of a torn hamstring. The Achilles tendon (it is not a muscle, but a strip of fibrous tissue which attaches a muscle to a bone) links the calf muscle to the heel. It is pretty strong, and most players will spend their entire careers blissfully unaware of the agony of a rupture. However, it is more vulnerable after a period of inactivity. Players returning from other injuries often find themselves sidelined after a couple of games with strains (or worse) to this important tendon.

Therefore, it is important to work on keeping this part of the body flexible this if we are home training. Fortunately, as with other stretches in this section, it is easy to do. Lean forward to touch a wall for support. Put one leg slightly in front of the other. (Heel to toe is fine with this exercise.) Bend the knee of the front leg. Keep the sole of the rear foot firmly on the floor. Lean forwards slowly – do not 'bounce'. When the Achilles stretches hold for ten seconds and relax. Repeat four or five times then swap legs.

Number Thirteen - Fitness Exercise: Lower Body Work Out

This drill is a good one to finish this section of the warmup on, as it works on multiple sets of muscles. For this, simply perform a lunge, ensuring the legs stay in place, then twist to one side then the other. Repeat five times and then swap legs. This drill helps to stretch the hamstrings, gluts, groin and quads, hips and lower back muscles. It should not be used in place of the individual exercises above but is a good way to enhance them as a final exercise in the lower body warm up.

Number Fourteen – Fitness Drill: On the Rebound (1)

Once we have stretched, we can move forward to getting the blood flowing and the heart pumping. When space is limited there is no better way than by making use of a rebounder (or, failing this, a wall) Try fifty first time passes with each foot.

Number Fifteen – Fitness Drill: On the Rebound (2)

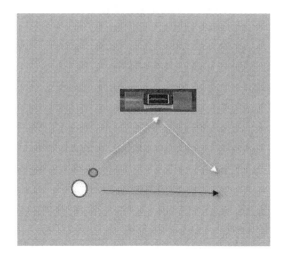

We can develop this by passing from level with the edge of the rebounder towards its center (see diagram above for clarity), then jog to the other end of the rebounder to receive the pass. Repeat in the opposite direction. Complete twenty circuits.

Stamina Building Exercises We Can Do at Home

Even though we might not be able to get to the gym, we can still set up workouts to do at home which will provide excellent cardiovascular workouts. As always, we recommend that people coming back from injury, who have been out of exercise for a while or who have existing respiratory, heart or other conditions take advice from a professional before beginning a campaign of exercise.

Number Sixteen - Fitness Exercise: Step Aerobics

Provided we don't live in a bungalow, there is bound to be a step in the house somewhere. Step aerobics are highly effective, easy to do and can be carried out while listening to music or watching TV. Thirty minutes per day is a good target, but that can be broken down into three slots of ten minutes without any loss to improvement in fitness.

Start simply, with a step up using one foot, the other foot joining its sibling on the step, then back downwards one step at a time. More complicated moves can be added later – there are plenty of videos online which can guide you in this.

Step aerobics is an excellent drill for soccer players because as well as aerobic exercise, several sets of muscles are worked on. Mostly, these are the legs and lower back muscles, which are crucial for a soccer player.

Number Seventeen - Fitness Exercise: Outdoor Home Circuit

Circuit training is a well-established fitness technique, allowing the user to focus on different muscle groups while building cardiovascular fitness. It will provide the following benefits:

- Body strengthening,
- Body conditioning,

- Can be adapted to support drills particularly useful for soccer players,
- Helps with weight low,
- Helps with stamina.

Circuits, though, by themselves, are not the perfect fitness exercise. Because they are particularly handy with burning fat, they are less useful to those whose body fat index is naturally low. Also, because several activities takes place, the actual work spent on any one particular muscle group is low. Circuits work best used to compliment other workouts.

Here is an eight-step circuit, which can be used inside and out, and which will give a particular focus on lower body muscles in addition to stamina development.

Ten Squats: Working the glutes, or buttock muscles. Body position is vital to get the maximum benefit from a squat.

- Stand with the feet a shoulder width apart,
- Point our toes slightly outwards,
- Lower the body carefully and under control so that we 'sit' between the space left by our legs,
- Ensure we look forward throughout the squat to keep the back straight,

- Make sure our knees extend no further than our toes. This will help reduce strain on the knee joint.
- Hold the position for a count of five,
- Slowly stand.

Two Minutes Skipping: Working the calf muscles.

- Keep both feet together,
- Jump over the rope,
- Bend the knees to lift the feet,
- Keep the feet together and land,
- Jump from the balls of the feet.

Twenty leg raises: This exercise works the abdominal muscles.

- Lay flat on the floor with arms by the side,
- Slowly raise the feet so that they reach an angle of 45 degrees,
- Keep the legs together, and straight,
- Hold for a count of three,
- Slowly lower.

Two-minute step aerobics: See the drill earlier.

Ten Back Stretches: This exercise is good for the lower back muscles.

- Lie flat on the floor, stomach down,

- Extend our arms forward, so that they brush the side of our head,
- Look forwards,
- Slowly lift our torso off the floor, hold for a count of three, then lower.

Two-minute-High Knee Jog: This entertaining (to watch, if not do) exercise works all of the leg muscles while also delivering good cardiovascular training.

It is an exercise that really does do what it says on the box. Simply jog lifting the knees as high as possible. Ensure that both legs work equally hard. An easy mistake is to lose concentration, and work only the stronger leg.

Twenty Shoe Box Jumps: This exercise works the calf and hip muscles. It is also good for balance.

- Place a shoe box on the floor, and stand next to it,
- Complete two footed jumps from side to side of the box.
- Keep our arms out to maintain balance.

Two-minute Sprint Relay: Excellent for replicating the high intensity sprints of a soccer match. Simply jog on the spot for twenty seconds, then make a high intensity sprint on the spot for ten seconds.

We would suggest three rotations of the circuit, although, of course, it is best to adapt the regime to our personal fitness levels and goals.

Number Eighteen – Exercise Drill: Don't Forget We're Soccer Players Circuit

High intensity work outs have their place when we cannot get a ball at our feet. However, soccer is the game we love, and where possible we want to include a ball in our drills. Out of respect for our granny's passed down glassware, we can't do that indoors. But we can in the back yard. Here is a suggested eight drill circuit using a ball. It will help to maintain fitness while being a little more entertaining to those who find individual exercise unmotivating.

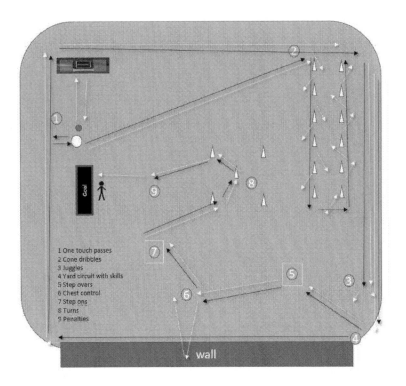

Twenty-Two-Touches:

- Use a wall or rebounder. Stay about 10 meters away

- Hit the ball against the wall with one foot,

- While the ball is travelling complete four 'mini jogs' on the spot,

- Control the ball with the same foot as the pass was made,

- In the control, position the ball to strike it against the wall with the weaker foot.

- On the final touch, turn and dribble to…

Four Cone Circuits:

- Have two rows of six cones laid out,
- Dribble in and out using both feet,
- Complete a turn, such as the Cruyff turn,
- Dribble back on the other set of cones,
- On finishing flick the ball up and…

Ten Juggles: Throw in five press ups every time the ball hits the floor.

Navigate the Yard:

- Run with the ball round the circumference of our yard.
- On each side, complete one skill, such as a step over or feint.

Thirty Super Step Overs:

- Stop the ball dead,
- Using arms for balance, and looking forwards – not down…
- Complete fifteen fast step overs with each foot, alternating between the feet.

10 Chest Control: We work as fast as we can on this drill.

- Dribble to the wall or rebounder,
- Pass firmly against the wall,
- On the rebound, flick the ball up and catch it,
- Make a throw in,

- Control the rebound on our chest, so the ball drops to our feet,
- Make the pass and repeat.

Thirty Step Ons:

- Alternating feet quickly touch the top of the ball with the bottom of our toes.

Ten Goalie Time Saves:

- Use the rebounder or wall to set up saves,
- Throw the ball so we need to dive to make the saves,
- Dive to alternate sides,
- Get to our feet as quickly as we can.

Ten Super Turns:

- Dribble to the small square end of the dribbling zone,
- Dribble from a corner to the center cone,
- Make a turn at the center cone, changing direction and dribble to a different corner cone,
- Repeat

Ten Penalties:

- Take the penalties, aiming for a different spot each time,
- Sprint to collect the ball after the penalty.

Complete two or three circuits for a really useful workout.

Number Nineteen – Drill Game: Garage Fives

Some of us fill our garage with every bit of junk that won't go indoors. If that is us, then this game won't really work. (A version can be adapted for a wall, and still provides some benefits in terms of agility, but not as good as the real thing.) However, some people keep their garage for their car, and that is a good idea. Because it means that if we back out and park on the drive for a bit, we have a very handy space in which we can play a version of the excellent game which is fives.

Rather like Real Tennis, Racquets and such like, Fives is a sport invented by the British and destined for undeserved obscurity. In fact, it began life in the great Public (by which, in the British sense, we mean private, fee paying) Schools. So, there is Eton Fives, Winchester Fives and Rugby Fives.

Eton is the most exciting form. The privileged boys sent by their parents to endure icy dormitories, severe beatings, inedible food and the uncertain attentions of their teachers (they call them 'Beaks' at Eton) in an attempt to prepare them for a life of abusing the poor and anybody whose skin was of a slightly different hue used to get very bored. The problem was, there were no walls at Eton flat enough to play with a ball against. Except one section on the outside of the Eton Chapel. This wall was handicapped by a raised area at the front, and step which linked it to a wider space, before another step took the worshippers back into the main 'Quad' area (a sort of enormous yard). Also, a ledge ran along the front of the wall, and into a buttress which projected somewhat annoyingly a short distance from the main wall, along a supporting structure.

But, hey ho, the boys were resourceful, and Fives was born. The game retains gloriously archaic terms, such as blackguard (a false serve), pepper pot (an area near the buttress from which, if the ball falls in, it cannot emerge) and step (a ritual by which the server is handicapped as they reach game point). But we do not need to worry about this. Nor do we need to worry about Chapels, Buttresses and ledges halfway up walls. Because shortly after Eton discovered their version of Fives, the chaps at Rugby School came up with Rugby Fives. Their motivation was perhaps a little different. Ever since little Webb Ellis had taken fright during a game of soccer (or football, as it is known in the public schools), picked up the ball and run away with it, they had a new game, Rugby. Unfortunately, the rate of serious injury caused by this particular game was starting to threaten not only Matron's sick bay, but the lives of the young players. Since the second most popular past time at Rugby appeared to be (judging by contemporary novels) roasting small boys over fires, unsurprisingly the smaller children began to look for a safer, more genteel sport. And rugby fives was born.

Fortunately for we self-isolating, lone soccer loving fitness addicts, the shape of a rugby fives court is remarkably similar to that of most American, Australian and European garages. It really doesn't matter if there is the odd shelf or heavy box is fixed to the walls, because these can just be used to add to the excitement. Our only warning is safety; both for the objects on the shelves (we come back to Grandma's glassware, or garden shears which might fall and cause a painful injury) and the players. Provided there is no risk, a great game can be had.

Fives is played using special padded gloves. Both hands are used and a cork, golf ball sized ball, is the object.

Fives can be played as a solo activity helping keep the body flexible and agile through the turning involved, or where allowed, as a pairs game. Because it uses the hands, it is relatively easy to play (but very difficult to master) and so is great for a Dad to play with their daughter, or a son to compete against his mom.

If playing competitively, we might want to draw a line across the width of the garage to create a step. A line around three meters from the end wall is fine, although the bigger the step, the faster the game.

We also use a line (for example, one drawn with chalk, or a line in the bricks, on the end wall above which the ball must hit.)

For a ball, since we have neither padded gloves nor axis to the single producer we believe exists somewhere in the dark recesses of a Muggle-led Diagon Allay, we suggest either an old tennis ball, or a high bouncing squash ball.

We can adapt rules to our circumstances. Playing solo, we can aim for as many hits as we can, volleying or on one bounce. We should look to alternate hand and use techniques similar to squash and tennis. We get low to the ball and play sideways on. In the diagram, we have shown a short rally, the black player's shots marked with grey lines for clarity.

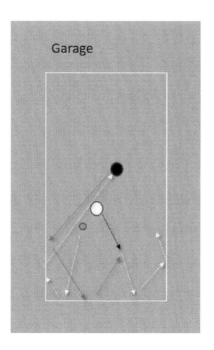

Here are some suggested rules for a pairs game:

- First to ten points,
- Points are won when the ball bounces beyond the step (point lost by hitter), goes out of the garage without bouncing (point lost), fails to hit the front wall (point lost) or bounces more than once (point won) or cannot be returned (point won).
- If the server wins the point, a score is made, for example, 1-0; if the non-server wins the point, there is no score added, but serve changes hand.
- The serve is made so that the ball hits the front wall, side wall then bounces on the 'step'.

- The serve is returned with the ball hitting the side wall, front wall and bouncing on the step.
- There is no point won or lost if the serve or the return fails to be legal. The serve is simply retaken.
- If the receiver does not like the serve, they may ask for it to be replayed.
- Once the serve and return are legal, the game is underway, and the point continues until it is won or lost.

This is a great little game, which really helps fitness and agility. It can be adapted for an open space using a wall. If in the garage, please take care to:

- Remove any object which might fall if hit, or if the player crashes into it,
- Do not play if any obstacles might present a danger, for example injuring an eye by running into a shelf,
- The ball travels fast, so do remove any breakables.

But for those whose garage is clear, except for maybe a high, empty and secure shelf or a box sitting safely in a corner, it is a perfect, competitive training exercise.

However, we can find other ways to help build stamina which incorporate everyday activities. They might not be quite as much fun as heading down to the gym, but since they offer the bonus of getting some mundane chores out of the way there is plenty of compensation for that particular loss.

Number Twenty - Fitness Exercise: Working Out is a Chore (literally)

Here are some ideas:

- Do the housework to music, working faster than usual.
- Dig that flower bed,
- Cut the grass at a jog.
- Sweep the yard to music.

Drills with Pop Up Goals

Our aim with these back-yard drills is to keep the number of players to a minimum. See the tips below for suggestions to achieve this, however we will present the drills with a maximum of four players in action. Each can be reduced to a minimum of one or two players with clever substitution.

Number Twenty-One - Tip: Pass or Shoot

A mannequin, or its equivalent, placed in front of a small pop up goal, or home-made goal, will help to make a drill more challenging. We can change the position of this 'fake keeper' to encourage us to shoot towards different parts of the goal.

Number Twenty-Two – Tip: A Bouncing Friend

We can make use of a rebounder or wall to represent a pass to and from a teammate. A bit like a one-two before shooting into the pop-up goal on the first touch.

Number Twenty-Three - Tip: Building a Defense

Mannequins can be used to represent defenders. Of course, their fundamental problem is, like some center backs, they are reluctant to move around. However, we can employ a second mannequin to represent the space to which a defender would, if they were real, relocate. So, dribble past two mannequins before shooting into the pop-up goal.

Number Twenty-Four - Drill: Decision Making

With those key tips out of the way, let us get on to some real soccer drills. Our aim in the first is to make good decisions regarding whether to dribble or pass to create the best shooting opportunity.

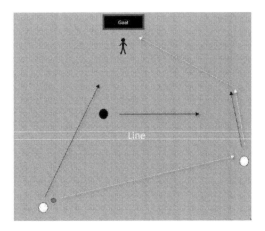

For this drill we need a pop up goal, two attackers – one who delivers the first pass and a team mate who receives it (as suggested above, the use of a wall or rebounder can replace this attacker if needs must); a keeper (or mannequin), a defender who will move (or two mannequins)

In terms of importance, after ourselves as the principle player comes the defender, then the attacking teammate, then lastly (as always, they will argue, but that is goalies for you) the keeper.

Our pitch is as big as we can make it, with a minimum of 20 meters by 15 meters. The pitch is divided into two with a middle line running across the width of the playing area. The two attacking players begin in the area furthest from the goal, with the defender in the defensive area.

A free pass is made, and from that point the defender may play anywhere in the defensive half of the pitch. (Note, if a rebounder is used to represent the second attacker, it should be placed on the halfway line, so it can be of most use as the drill develops). Attackers may play anywhere on the pitch. When in possession, the player chooses whether to dribble to create space for a shot or make the pass.

The key skills in play here are:

- Decision making,
- Accuracy of passing,
- First touch,
- The ability to employ dribbling skills,
  - Change of direction,
- Shooting.

The key criteria for decision making are:

- Quality of first touch,
- Position of defense,
- Difficulty of shooting position,
- Position of teammate.

There is another factor here, possibly. Some readers may have followed podcasts made during the pandemic by the BBC's long running but temporarily redundant soccer show, Match of the Day. In one podcast, three of England's finest ever strikers – Alan Shearer, Ian Wright and Gary Lineker – discussed the mentality required to be a great goal scorer.

A degree of selfishness was something on which they all agreed. Not blind tunnel vision, but a sense that, as striker, they will always score and therefore a teammate must be in an unequivocally better position in order for them to make a pass rather than take the ball on themselves. It is a point to bear in mind.

Number Twenty-Five - Drill: Agility Shooting

The aim here is to improve shooting quality after direction changes.

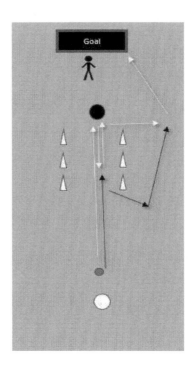

This drill works best with a striker (white), pivot player (black) and keeper (mannequin), but can be played with just the striker and a rebounder which replaces the pivot. However, the drill becomes slightly different in its penultimate stage if there is no human pivot player.

We require cones, ball and pop up goal. A minimum playing area of 20 meters by 10 meters is needed. The pitch is marked out with a channel made of cones.

Using a human pivot, the drill works as follows: the striker plays a pass into the pivot and runs on towards the channel. The pivot returns

42

a pass. The striker plays a second pass into the pivot, but this time changes direction by back pedaling towards the beginning of the channel.

The striker now indicates which side they would like the final pass to be played and run on to an angled pass played in this direction by the pivot. They shoot first time.

If the pivot is replaced with a rebounder, the striker has one of two options.

1) The second pass is played at an angle, so it is returned at an angle. The striker still back pedals, and then runs onto the angled pass, takes a touch if necessary, and shoots.
2) The second pass is played straight. The striker back pedals, receives the return pass from the rebounder and dribbles to one side or other before shooting. In order to work on the weaker foot, the striker should alternate the direction of the dribbles.

The key skills being developed are:

- Passing accurately into feet,
- First touch,
- Changing direction,
- Shooting first time.

Number Twenty-Six – Tip: Shooting Across the goal

43

The drill above requires shooting low and across the goal. With a small pop up goal, extra zones can be added either side of the goal. The striker aims to score in the far version, depending on the side from which they are shooting, of these additional zones.

Number Twenty-Seven - Drill: Dribble and Shoot

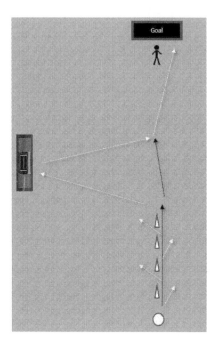

This is another agility shooting drill which can be played in a back yard. An area 25 meters by 10 meters is required, with a pop-up goal at one end. This drill can be practiced alone, or with teammates. Our aim is to combine three skills essential for an attack minded player, dribbling, passing and shooting, in order to create a goal scoring chance.

44

A line of cones is set up, three meters apart. A rebounder (or teammate) is positioned to one side.

Simply dribble through the cones, play a one two with the teammate or rebounder and shoot first time. Aim to keep shots down and play them across the keeper to the far corner.

The key skills we are working on here are:

- Dribbling skills at speed,
- Accurate passing,
- Running on to return passes,
- Adjusting the body to shoot first time.

Number Twenty-Eight - Tip: Varying the Return Pass from a Rebounder

To make the use of a rebounder more realistic to a match situation, try either chipping a pass into it, or striking a low pass hard so it bounces off the metal base frame of the tool(where the design incorporates one). These options will lead to a return pass which is bouncing or bobbling and can be used to improve first touch to a bouncing ball or shooting on the volley or half volley.

Number Twenty-Nine - Tip: Shooting Straight against a Keeper

When we are shooting from wide, we usually aim to striker with the laces, through the ball with the head over it. This imparts power while keeping the ball low. We should aim for the far post, so any touch the keeper gets on the ball can direct it towards a teammate. A keeper will also look to cover their near post more fully than the far post.

When the return pass comes straight into the middle of the goal, we can get good results from changing our shooting style. We look to take one touch, so the keeper is unsure whether we are planning to shoot or dribble. We shoot hard and low closer to the keeper's body, because there is a very tight angle to find a corner. We shoot early, before the keeper is set, and strike powerfully with the instep for accuracy. We open our bodies up to disguise the placement of the shot.

Number Thirty - Drill: Turn and Shoot

This is a particularly good drill for solo practice. The aim is to turn quickly and shoot. It requires a rebounder and a pop-up goal, a playing area at least 20 meters in length and while it will work with just one ball, a larger collection makes the drill more worthwhile.

During the drill we will practice a number of turns. For more details of these, see the penultimate chapter on close ball control skills.

We stand with our back to goal, facing the rebounder (a human player can also fulfil this role). We play a pass into the rebounder and position ourselves on the half turn ready for the pass, receive the return, turn quickly and shoot. If we have enough balls not to have to retrieve the shot immediately, we repeat the exercise quickly, working hard at pace.

We should aim to try a number of different turns, working in both directions to help develop our weaker side, and look to get our shots away quickly.

The skills we are developing in this drill are

- Receiving a pass on the half turn,
- Turning quickly,
- Turning using different techniques,
- Shooting first time with power and accuracy.

Let us finish this chapter with a small collection of fun games which we can play or teach to our kids.

Number Thirty-One - Drill: One per Side 2 v 2 or more

This game makes use of whatever equipment we have to hand which can be used to represent extra players. We need two pop up goals (or equivalent) and whatever other equipment we lends itself to the drill. A rebounder sits to one side on the halfway line. If we have a wall we can use as well, then this makes a touch line we can use as we would in a five a side indoor game and be available for wall passes.

Players can position mannequins in the best place they think, such as a goalkeeper, or a central defender.

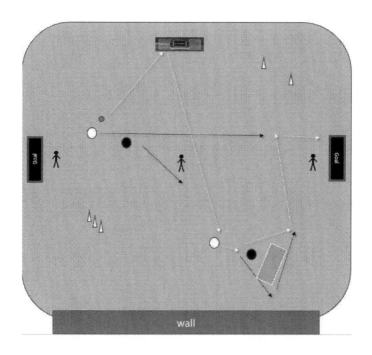

When the pitch is set up, we play a 1 v 1 game, using the equipment to support our effort.

On top of ball skills, here we are helping to develop endurance and fitness.

Number Thirty-Two - Drill: Target Practice

For this drill, we need a pop-up goal and a ball. If we are playing competitively, then each player requires a ball.

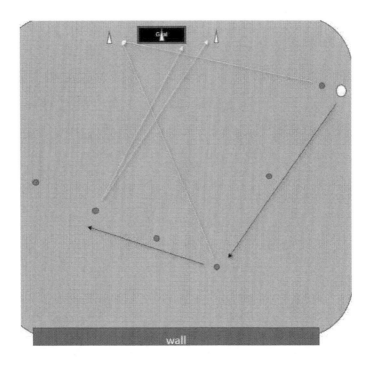

Set a number of shooting positions around the back yard. Divide the goal into three zones – center, near post and far post. If the pop-up goal is particularly small, then add wide zones either side.

Then shoot from the various positions. These positions are marked as grey dots. Near post score is worth one point, a central shot is worth two, and a far post shot for three. The drill can be made more challenging by placing obstructions, such as empty shoe boxes, in front of the goal, requiring a shot to be firm enough to knock the obstructions out of the way.

Key skills here are shooting with accuracy and power.

Number Thirty-Three - Drill: Juggle and shoot

Here we combine the close individual skills of juggling with shooting. Players start 10 meters from the goal. A time limit is set, say five minutes. Players must complete ten juggles then shoot without taking a touch.

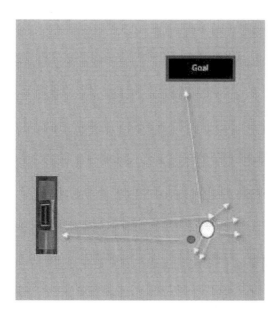

If they score, they receive a point. If they miss, they must start the juggles again. If the ball hits the ground during a juggle sequence, they may restart the juggle from the point it went wrong. For example, if they are on six juggles when they make a mistake, they resume on six, requiring just four more before they can shoot.

Here we are practicing the key skills of ball dexterity and shooting. More skilled players can begin with a return pass from the rebounder, from which they begin their juggle.

Number Thirty-Four - Tip: Competing with Our Kids

If we are spending a lot of time at home, there is nothing like getting out and playing soccer with our kids. The problem can come if matters become too competitive. Try introducing handicap systems to even things up, for example in a shooting contest starting from different positions or making goals of different sizes.

That way, with the handicap weighted in our favor, there is a chance we might beat our ten-year-old in a game or two.

Number Thirty-Five - Drill: Three and In

A really simple, tradition game for two players. One plays as keeper, the other as outfield player. Score three goals and swap roles. To make the game more fun, and add interest, try the following variations:

- Keeper can only use their hands and body, not feet or legs,
- Play with a tennis ball, beach ball or sponge ball for variation,
- Keeper stays on their knees.

As we will see as the book develops, there is no claim that such drills are as exciting or complex as the sort we might use in a full training session. Our aim is to make maximum use of the resources at our disposal, helping to develop our skills and maintain our fitness in challenging circumstances.

Drills with Rebounders

This is a great piece of equipment which will transform the range of drills we can practice in our yards. Perhaps the biggest benefit a tool such as this brings to the home training soccer player is that it allows team drills to be worked on by the individual. Since soccer is, more than anything else, a team sport, such an advantage is worth its weight in goals.

Without something like a rebounder, those skills essential to soccer – passing, heading (for older ages and adult players), touch and, to a lesser extent, shooting are very hard to develop. However, the rebounder brings into play the necessary repetition required to water these key elements of our game and encourage them to grow.

Number Thirty-Six - Drill: Fifty-One Touch Passes

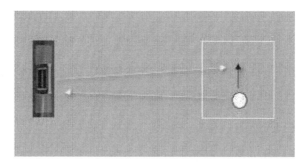

A very simple drill to begin. But still one which not only helps with warm up, but also helps the player to get the 'feel' of a well weighted pass. All that is needed is the rebounder, a ball and a small marked 5-meter square grid, five to ten meters (depending on difficulty level) in front of the rebounder.

The player plays 10 first time passes with one foot, switches to the other, repeats and plays the final ten passes hit with the outside of the foot, alternating feet. The player must stay inside the grid to play the passes.

Key skills here are:

- Weighting the pass,
- Moving quickly into position to play the next pass first time,
- Remember key body position – arms out for balance, on toes, striking the ball with the instep or outside of foot, on the half turn as the ball comes.

Number Thirty-Seven - Drill: Volley Passing with a Rebounder

We can make this drill harder by trying volley passes. The key skills we will be developing are:

- Angling our body to the side, with arms for balance,
- Striking the ball with the laces,
- Smooth follow through,
- Aim slightly to the side for accuracy, as the ball will naturally curve away from the angle of the leg.

55

Look to catch the ball and repeat. The drill can be made more challenging by starting with a normal pass off the ground, and then playing the volley after the bounce on the return.

Number Thirty-Eight - Tip: Angling the Rebounder

Try experimenting with positioning the rebounder at different angles to increase the difficulty of receiving return passes.

Number Thirty-Nine - Tip: Multiple Rebounders

Where facilities and equipment allow, set up drills (such as the following one) using multiple rebounders and a wall.

Number Forty - Drill: Drill Square

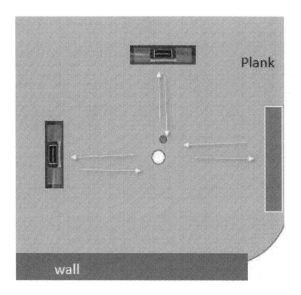

This drill does require a little more equipment than most. We have assumed two rebounders, a wall and a solid wooden plank from the garage to make the fourth side of the square.

We create a twenty-meter square using the equipment and wall. A smaller square works if space is limited. The drill involves playing return passes off the rebounders and their makeshift equivalent, receiving the ball, turning ninety or one hundred and eighty degrees, and making a pass to another side.

The key skills we will be developing here are:

- Passing firmly and accurately using the instep,
- Control on the half turn,
- Changing direction on control,

We should look to stay lightly on our toes, keep our arms out for balance, and cushion the ball as it comes off the rebounders or walls in order to help develop our technique.

Number Forty-One - Tip: Using Technology for Technique

Normally, our coaches and teammates will be there to advise us on technique. If we are practicing alone, that help is missing. It is easy to slip into bad habits, particularly when we are repeating drills and exercise.

Setting up our phone and switching it to record will allow us to check out our technique. We drill for two minutes, check the phone video for our technique, if good we continue the exercise. If our technique is wrong, then we adjust, record again, check and continue when we have it right.

The final chapter of our book contains tips and guidance on key techniques in soccer.

Number Forty-Two - Drill: Controlling A High Ball (1)

By throwing the ball at the rebounder, we can create accurate high return passes to us.

For this drill we simply require a ball and a rebounder. Plus, of course, ourselves. The drill involves throwing the ball against the rebounder, then controlling the return. We then bring the ball down and pass back to the rebounder using our feet. As the ball is returned, we collect it and repeat the exercise.

We should use our feet to get into position quickly so that we can control the ball on our chest.

Key Skills we will be developing in this drill are:

- Moving quickly into position to allow us time to control the ball,
- Keeping arms out for balance and protection,

- Chest big, and protect the ball with the body as it drops,
- Weighting the first-time pass.

Number Forty-Three - Drill: Controlling a High Ball (2)

We repeat drill number forty-two, but this time work on controlling the ball with the thigh.

The skills we are developing are:

- Moving quickly into position,
- Raising the receiving thigh so that the ball drops about halfway between the top and the knee,
- Cushioning slightly to allow the ball to drop,
- Head still during procedure,
- Weighting the pass.

Number Forty-Four - Drill: Taking a Throw In

Throw ins are an increasingly important part of the game. No longer is it just about a restart; with the fast pass counter attacking of modern soccer, losing possession from a throw can put a team in trouble, and control of the throw thus becomes extremely important.

Equally, a traditional long throw can turn a defense and create an attacking opportunity.

We can use the rebounder to practice both throw in and receiving the throw. Throw in from distance to improve strength and accuracy, throw from closer to improve control of the return.

Twenty throw ins, from four different positions, will allow us to practice the following key skills:

- Accuracy in throw ins,
- Long Throw ins,
- Controlling the return with different parts of the body,
- Moving into position to receive the return quickly.

The technique for a long throw involves a short run up, both feet are planted firmly behind the 'line', the back arches and the ball – held firmly in two hands, as close to each other as control will allow. The ball is launched forwards with a springing action from both arms and released just short of the vertical with a final flick of the wrists. Release too early and too much height will be gained, too late and the ball will just bounce into the ground.

Real long throw experts develop a 'flat' throw, one which has little arch in it, but instead speeds in on a relatively flat trajectory. Considerable upper body strength, allied to good technique, is required to deliver this. Beware of straining back muscles when attempting this.

Number Forty-Five - Tip: Errors with Young Players

Very young players find throwing in difficult. This is because they have not developed the co-ordination to perform all of the various moves simultaneously and with control. Consider, the feet need to come together, as the arms rotate from behind the back while keeping hold of a large (relative to small hands) sphere, a spring must be injected into the arms as the ball comes forward. Release needs to be at the perfect point and allied to a flick of a wrists.

Two common mistakes for young players is for one foot to flick into the air on release, resulting in a foul throw or for the ball to spin out of the hands, and go nowhere.

The first error is caused by the young player attempting to throw the ball too far. Encourage distance to come from technique rather than power. The second is because the small hands of the player mean that they are holding the ball too much on opposite sides. Encourage the player to get their hands behind the ball as much as possible, even if this means they can only throw it a short distance.

Number Forty-Six - Drill: Heading Challenge

We must be wary of heading drills. Research is beginning to demonstrate a link between later life dementia and heading the ball. The unfortunate condition is three or four times more prevalent in ex soccer players than the general population.

The following two drills are recommended to be played using a dry sponge ball, or light ball. Failing this, only adults should attempt them, and then only one of the drills in a particular session, and for no more than five repetitions.

Set the pop-up goal at right angles to the rebounder. Starting from outside the far post from the rebounder, throw downwards two handed to create a floating bounce. Run onto the ball and aim to rise above it, heading downwards.

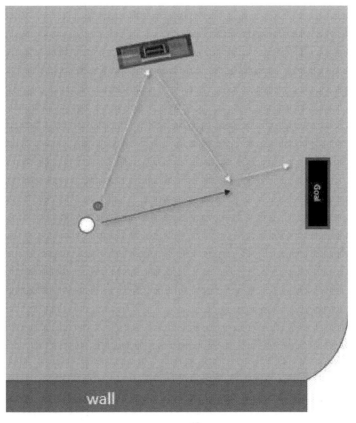

Key Skills:

- Time the run and jump so that we meet the ball as high as we comfortably can, but not too high so that we cannot get above the ball to head downwards,
- Head with the center of the forehead, twisting the neck on impact to direct the ball,
- Use the neck muscles to thrust the head forwards at impact, generating power,
- Use arms out for balance and protection.

Number Forty-Seven - Drill: Diving in the Spectacular

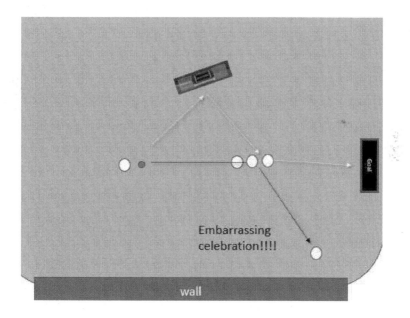

63

Nothing is more fun than a diving header. For this drill, start in line with the far post of the pop-up goal, relative to the rebounder. Take a couple of steps and throw the ball under arm at the rebounder. Ensure the ball is released at an angle, so the rebound is angled forward. (It may take a few attempts to get the ball delivery right, here.)

Continue running on to the ball, and time the dive to strike the ball with the forehead while in mid-flight.

Perform a spectacular celebration if the ball flies into the net.

Number Forty-Eight - Tip: Throwing at the Rebounder

To get the best out of the rebounder, it is worth spending a few minutes examining what happens with different throws. Accuracy is best achieved with a double handed under arm throw. A goalkeeper's 'bowl' throw will generate height and loop on the return. A double handed overarm throw, downwards and with power will lead to a powerful return, with less loop in its arc.

Number Forty-Nine - Drill: Goalkeeping

A good and fun way to learn about the effect of throws on the rebounder is to combine trials with a goalkeeping drill. (for children, definitely, but adults also enjoy throwing themselves around. Especially if they can justify it!).

Set a goal opposite the rebounder and throw from between the two. Try to save the rebounds. The angle of the rebounder can also be changed to generate harder saves.

Key Skills:

- Stand lightly on the toes, with knees bent and arms slightly forwards and out,
- Have the fingers of our hands pointing upwards?
- Bounce gently on the toes, bending the knees slightly on the bounce,
- When diving, kick hard off the opposite foot to the direction of the dive,
- Keep an eye on the ball throughout the dive,
- If catching, keep the fingers upwards and bring the ball into the body on making the catch,
- If palming away, keep the wrists lock to stop the ball powering through the hand,
- Palm away from the goal, ideally behind for a corner.

A little tip, since there will be some spectacular tips over the bar with this drill, don't place the goal too close to the yard fence. Our neighbors might get a little fed up with returning lost soccer balls…especially if they must pick them out of the remains of their petunias.

Number Fifty - Drill: Shoot and Save

This drill builds on the one above. Instead of throwing the ball, we shoot hard into the rebounder, then quickly get in position to save the rebound.

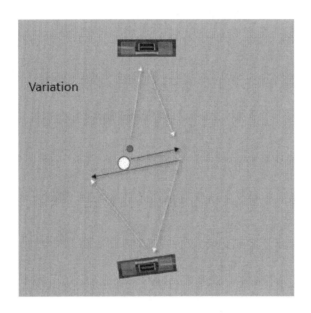

Set up a goal and rebounder approximately ten to fifteen meters apart. Start two thirds of the way back to the goal.

Shoot at the rebounder and look to save the rebound. Work hard on getting into position quickly in order to be best placed to make the save.

The drill can be developed by changing the angle of the rebounder or shooting from wider positions giving more ground to cover to make the save.

Another variation uses two rebounders. Here the player stands halfway between the rebounders, shoots, saves and turns quickly to shoot off the opposite rebounder.

Key skills:

- Shooting with power and accuracy using the laces,
- Moving quickly into position,
- Bending knees, arms up and ready, lightly balanced on toes.

Since the ball travels more quickly with a shot compared to a throw, we need to move our feet much more rapidly to get into position with this adaptation of the drill. It replicates a match situation where a keeper has just made a save with their feet and needs to recover quickly for a follow up shot.

Number Fifty-One - Tip: The Importance of Repetition

We would be attempting to pull the wool over soccer player's eyes if we tried to claim that a backyard training session is as valuable as a full on, trainer led gathering. However, with rebounder practices one element important to our development as players can really be used. And that is repetition.

We gave a reminder, in tip forty-one, of the importance of good technique, especially when we do not have someone to watch us. Provided our technique is good for the drills we undertake, the repetition that is an inevitable part of using a rebounder will train our muscles to respond properly to situations on the pitch. We will automatically weight a pass, automatically get in position to receive one, for example.

Thirty or forty repetitions of each drill, two or three times per week, will see our individual training sessions really deliver results.

At the same time, if our technique is poor, we will be training our muscles to respond incorrectly to situations. We will automatically, in the pressure of a match, adopt the wrong body position to receive a pass, or strike it with wrong part of the foot.

Used properly, repetition is a boon. Incorrectly applied, it can become a handicap.

Hopefully this chapter has demonstrated that, of all the equipment we can purchase for back yard training sessions, a rebounder is among the most important. It becomes a teammate, and tool which can widen the variety of drills we can undertake and create opportunities for creative use of the space we have available.

When Friends Come Around for a Game

During the current pandemic, many countries have instigated various degrees of lockdown rules. However, some are allowing limited contact between friends and family. The following set of drills are designed for players who are able to work with a partner, either because there is a brother, mother, or other parents, sibling and relative in the home, or because they are permitted a friend to come over.

However, in keeping with good practice, the drills are always also designed to allow players to remain at least two meters apart .

Number Fifty-Two - Drill: Pass and Move

A handy drill for improving awareness of teammates and changing the direction of a pass.

For this drill we need two rows of four cones with each of the cones five meters apart. Then gap between the two lines of cones is ten meters, and halfway between them are two more cones five meters apart.

The drill begins with first time passing between the two central cones. After the ball has been passed **at least four times** one of the players chooses to move to one of the outside cones. The partner then changes the angle of the pass. The player who has moved dribbles

70

behind the cones, until in line with the central cones, and the drill is repeated.

The 6 numbers in the diagram represent the 6 lines where the ball is passed.

Try to avoid alternating which player moves wide, instead we communicate with the eyes to show that we are about to change positions.

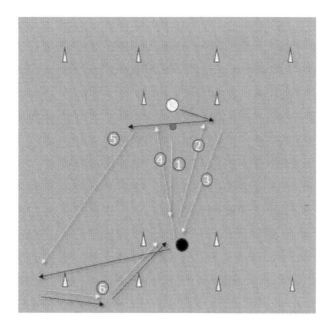

(For clarity, in this complicated diagram we have listed the order of passes.)

Key Skills in this drill are:

- Accurate and sympathetic first time passing, along the ground and with the instep to aid control,
- Staying on toes and alert,
- Back pedaling at pace to change position,
- Shifting body position quickly to play an angled pass.

Number Fifty-Three - Drill: Four Post

A variant on the drill above, here we have a 10 meters square with a cone in each corner. Players must pass between any two cones, into the square, but the ball must exit between the pair where the player begins. The drill thereby encourages movement to create space, change of body angles, and communication.

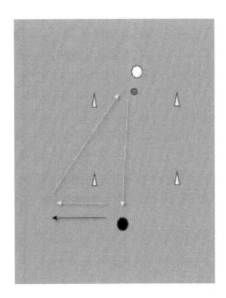

Number Fifty-Four - Drill: Four Past Variant

We can develop this drill with the following variant. Here, when the ball is passed, the receiver plays a first touch to take the ball between a different pair of cones, jogs around the nearest cone and plays a pass as in the drill above.

More movement by the receiving player is then encouraged, helping them to create new angles from which to play the pass. Players must also work hard to get back into position to receive their next pass.

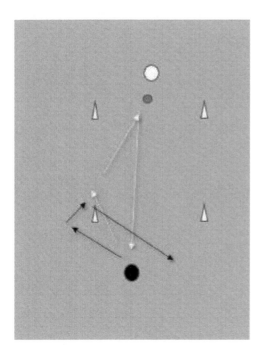

Number Fifty-Five - Drill: Four Post Change the Angle

Our final variant on this simple but effective drill requires the receiver to create space by controlling the ball to shift it 90 degrees laterally, to outside of the cones, before passing through the pair of cones to which his or partner is running.

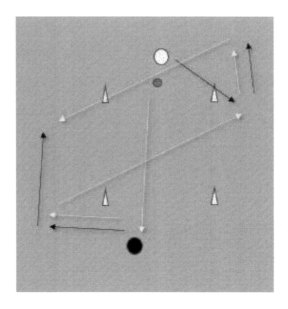

- The player must move their body to open it up to direct the first touch,
- Options to control the first pass include:
  - Rolling the studs over the ball to shift it sideways,
  - Controlling with the outside of the foot,
  - Allowing the ball to pass onto the rear foot and using the instep to change direction,

- As above, but hooking the rear foot to drag the ball in the opposite direction to where an instep control would take it,
- Body position is important in receiving the pass. Get on the half turn to allow options regarding which foot receives the ball. This will help to fool defenders

Number Fifty-Six - Drill: Chipping Drill

We need the full extremities of our 30 meters by 30-meter back yard for this drill. We set a rectangle at either end, 10 meters by 3 meters. The aim is to chip the ball from one box to the other. We can place an object in the middle to make the challenge more difficult, such as a rebounder or goal.

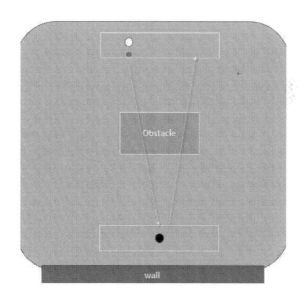

The technique we employ is as follows:

- Place non kicking foot beside and slightly, very slightly, behind the ball,
- Approach from a slight angle, strike the ball with the top of the instep/big toe, hitting the ball low down,
- Lean back slightly,
- Keep head still while striking the ball,
- Follow through smoothly to ensure the ball clears the obstacle.

Repeat ten times each, then develop the drill with some of the ideas number fifty-seven below.

Key Skills:

- Chipping the ball,
- Controlling using the relevant part of the body.

Number Fifty-Seven - Drill: Long Passing

We can develop the drill above in the following ways:

- Firm passing along the ground
  - Plant the non-kicking foot,
  - Strike with the instep,
  - Keep the head over the ball,
  - Follow through firmly,

- o The ball should curve slightly with the movement of the striking leg.
- Curled pass with outside of the foot
  - o Plant the non-kicking foot,
  - o Strike firmly with the outside of the boot,
  - o Follow through with a high lift,
  - o Keep head still, and arms out for balance
  - o We can place an obstacle mid-way in the passing area to curve the ball around.
- Driven pass with laces,
  - o Plant the non-kicking foot firmly beside the ball,
  - o Strike through the ball with laces,
  - o Bend the knee and keep the head forward so that the ball stays low.

Number Fifty-Eight - Drill: Controlled Volley Passing

Divide the width of the yard into three equal zones. Place an obstacle, such as a badminton net, tape on posts or even a pop-up goal in the middle of the central zone.

Volley pass to either end. Try various forms of volleying.

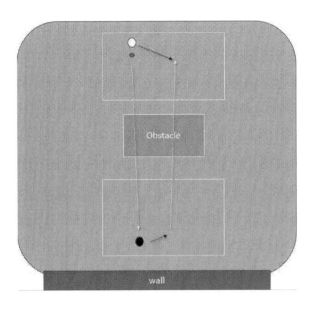

These can include:

- Side foot volleys, often used by defensive players making a clearance,
    - Get sideways to the ball, non-kicking leg forwards,
    - Watch the ball onto the rear foot, getting into position as quickly as possible,
    - Aim to strike the ball between shin and knee height,
    - Keep arms out for balance and head still,
    - Strike with the instep, using a smooth action,
    - Lean back on impact,
    - We are looking for height and distance in this volley.
- Screw kick volley, where it is important to make contact with the ball as early as possible,

- o Adopt the same positioning as above,
- o Strike the ball with the laces of the advanced foot,
- o This volley will potentially travel further but is harder to control.
- Side Volley, or goalkeeper's kick,
  - o Here we position to the side of a dropping ball,
  - o Lean away from the ball, using the hands for balance,
  - o Drive through the ball with the top of the laces,
  - o The ball should travel flat, and good accuracy can be found.

Number Fifty-Nine - Drill: Pass and score

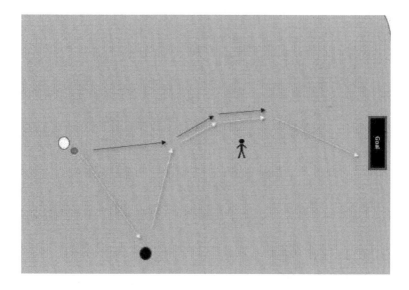

Here we seek to get the buildup play right before scoring in the empty goal. Position the pop-up goal to the side of the yard. Place a mannequin approximately 15 meters from the goal. Play a return pass with the teammate, beat the mannequin and shoot.

Repeat ten times then swap roles. This drill works well with multiple balls.

Key skills we are working on include:

- First time passing with accuracy,
- Dribbling to beat a defender,
- Shooting with accuracy.

Number Sixty - Drill: Shoot and Score with Players

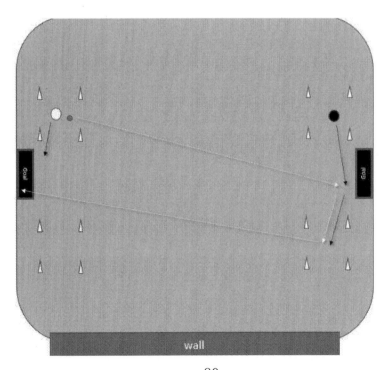

Two goals are required for this. Place goals at either end of the yard, marked out with a small penalty area, and take it in turns to shoot from distance from each player's own area.

Variations can be added to the game by having two areas either side of the goal, with players only able to move in front of their goal after the shot has been taken. Penalties can be introduced, for example, if the shot is too wide, or too high, a free penalty result.

First to score ten wins.

Number Sixty-One - Drill: Three Cone

In fact, we need four cones for this fast and energetic drill. One is fifteen meters away from the other three, which are placed in a triangle formation. The receiver starts behind the furthest cone. A pass is made towards either of the more advanced cone. The receiver moves forward to hit a return pass from the advanced cone, then back pedals to the rear cone in order to prepare for the next pass.

Key skills:

- Moving to receive a pass,
- Passing first time with the instep.

Number Sixty-Two - Drill: Backpedal and Shoot

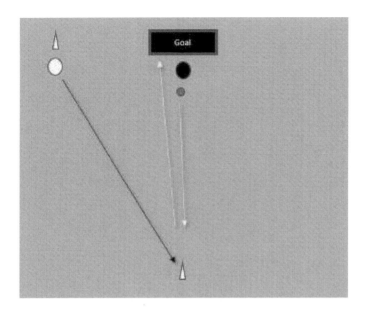

This is a great drill for encouraging strikers to back pedal to get into a shooting position. It works well with multiple balls but can be played with one.

A cone is placed 5 meters to the side of the goal, and another ten meters in front of the goal. The player starts by the forward cone, and back pedals to the central one. Meanwhile, the other player, acting as keeper, passes straight towards the central cone.

The striker must get into position and shoot first time. The drill is then repeated, with the goalkeeper retrieving the ball if necessary.

The drill can be developed by changing the position of the central cone to change the angle of the back pedal, and also the shot.

Number Sixty-Three - Drill: Headers and Volleys.

And why not? Brilliant for kids, it is what they would play down the park. And we are all kids at heart. (At least, we should be.) Just remember to keep that two-meter distance from each other.

Fun Soccer Based Games

Most of the games in this chapter can be played by single players, one v one or small teams. They are designed to develop soccer skills whilst offering a competitive alternative to a normal match.

Number Sixty-Four - Drill: Soccer Darts (using targets)

For this game, three balls are needed (although, we can manage with one), a target net across the goal (see the tip for homemade targets if we do not have one of these). Place a cone ten meters from the target. This is the 'oche', the line from which out football dart is kicked.

A value is given to each target; make the hardest worth 60 points, then down to 30 points. Ten points are awarded for hitting the goal, but not putting the ball through a target. No points are awarded if the attempt misses the goal.

Starting from 300 points, players take it in turns to have three shots. In order to begin scoring and end the game a score made through a target (rather than just hitting the goal) must be made.

The game is good for developing accuracy in passing and chipping.

Tip and Drill Number Sixty-Five: Coconut Shy

A fun accuracy game. Collect objects such as cans, plastic soda bottles and a one-gallon jerrycan. Fill them with water for stability. Create a series of levels using tables, plastic crates etc. Award a number of points to each object, more points for the harder it is to knock over.

Set a cone from which the player must make his shots. Points are scored each time an object is knocked over. The aim is to score the maximum number of points in ten shots.

Although this game takes a little while to set up, once it is done, it can be played quickly and without too much resetting. It is very popular with young players.

Again, it develops accuracy in passing and, since some of the objects will need to be hit with force to knock them down, shooting.

Number Sixty-Six - Drill: Soccer Show Jumping

This is a drill cum game which is good for younger children. It combines agility with soccer skills. It is basically an obstacle course with ten 'fences'. These fences can be agility tests, such as passing through a ladder, or soccer-based ones, such as shoot a goal from a penalty. We can shape the difficulty level of the course depending on the age of our players. The aim is to complete the course as quickly as possible. Each failure at a task generates four faults. A zero faults run with a slow time beats any time with four faults, and so on.

Here are ten suggested 'fences'

1) Dribble through cones. Run on to…
2) Play a return pass from the rebounder. Run on to…
3) Score a goal and leave the ball. Run on to…
4) Sprint through a ladder. Run on to…
5) Five juggles with a new ball, placed ready. Run on to…
6) Run with the ball between two cones. Run on to…
7) Five saves throwing the ball at the rebounder. Run on to…
8) Dribble through three mannequins and score. Leave the ball. Run on to…
9) Sprint between two cones 10m apart. Run on to…
10) Run up and score a penalty.

Here is a sample course.

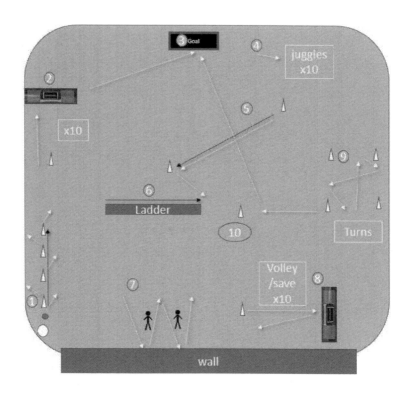

Number Sixty-Seven - Drill: Head Tennis

Given the warnings around about potential long-term consequences from heading the ball, we recommend that this game is played with a sponge ball or light beach ball. Set up a court 20 meters by 10 meters, with a badminton net, tape across two posts or series of plastic boxes etc. to represent the net.

Serve by throwing the ball up and heading it. The other player then has up to three juggles to control and return the ball. They may use their hands once (to help rallies develop), but only to flick the ball, not catch it. The move that sends the ball over the net must be a header.

Score as in tennis.

Number Sixty-Eight - Drill: Soccet

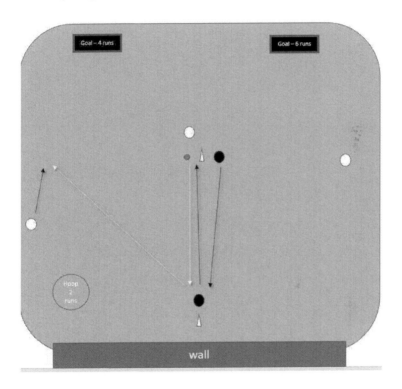

A minimum of two players is needed for this game, but if more are available, then the game becomes more fun. Therefore, it is ideal for a family to play together.

Set up a wicket. This means two mannequins approximately 15 meters apart. If there are enough players (minimum four) then there are two 'batsmen'. However, the game does work with solo batsmen.

Batsmen nominate a playing leg and foot. This could be marked by wearing a band or shin pad. The bowler attempts to hit the mannequin with a chip, shot or curved pass. The batsman attempts to protect the wicket with their torso, head or kicking foot. They may not use their hands, arms or the non-kicking foot.

Runs are scored by:

1) The batsman/men run between the mannequins. (One run for each length completed).
2) Specific areas score particular amounts of runs. For example, hitting the fence might be worth two runs, scoring a goal worth four, stopping the ball in a hoop laid down is worth six.

Players are out if:

1) The ball hits their mannequin.
2) The mannequin to which they are running is hit by the ball before they reach it.
3) A shot they hit is caught by an opponent before it hits the ground.

4) The ball hits their non kicking leg, arm or hand AND would have hit their mannequin otherwise.

5) The ball is kicked over the garden fence. If Mr Miserable Moaner is sitting in his backyard having a cup of coffee, it might be that the entire team is out!

Number Sixty-Nine - Drill: Kill Ball

This is an accuracy kicking game. We set up two lines of cones to mark the playing area. The lines are 20 meters apart. A ball is placed in the middle of the playing area. Players take it in turns to kick another ball, aiming to hit the target ball so it rolls over their opponent's line. Players may shoot from anywhere provided they are behind their line. They may not touch the target ball with any part of their body.

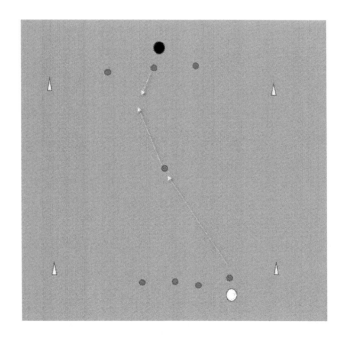

We can play a variation with multiple balls. Here, tactics come into play. Players may kick their balls when they wish. So, they could build up a supply and wait for their opponent to run out, then shoot several times quickly. Or, they might save a ball to act as a 'goalkeeper to stop a ball rolling towards their line.

Number Seventy - Drill: Soccer Golf

Set up holes in the back yard. Hoops represent the holes. We can set tees and lay down obstacles to get in the way. This is a fun game, kids will love it especially, and there are infinite varieties we can add using our imagination and the equipment we have to hand. We could even make a water hazard with a paddling pool. With creativity, a thirty by thirty-meter yard should easily provide room for six holes (two on each end, plus one on each side).

Number Seventy-One - Drill: Ten Pin Shooting and So Forth

It is worth making a collection of two-liter soda bottles. Half fill them with water, set them up as in a bowling alley, and away we go with soccer bowls.

Or we can play soccer crown green bowling. If we have an opponent (this works best as a competitive game) and half a dozen or eight soccer balls, then we are away. Roll a tennis ball at least 10 meters, or further. Take it in turns to try to kick our ball closest to this 'jack'. We can try curve passes to swing round an opponent, driven shots to knock opponents out of the way, chips and lay short blockers. Nearest ball to the jack scores. If the same player also has the second closest, they score two points and so on. Play ten ends. Take it in turns to roll the jack, so we can vary the length on which we play.

Soccer Boule is another variation. See diagram below. Set some boxes to make a low 'block', then a hoop another ten meters on. Players aim to stop a ball in the hoop (five points), bounce through the hoop (three points), be closest to the hoop (one point). Shots must be chipped over the barrier, and back spin imparted to stop the ball running away afterwards.

Number Seventy-Two - Drill: Dexterity

We are likely to have quite a lot of time on our own during lockdown periods. (Out of these, there are still times when become listless and look for something active to do.) We can build up our dexterity with a ball by simply trying tricks. Try catching the ball on our backs, juggle from foot to foot or back flick it over our heads. Such activity might seem a little mindless, but all the time we are developing our balance, our control of the ball and our physical dexterity.

Kids love to try these kinds of tricks indoors. Give them a balloon, a challenge, and away they go.

Dribbling and Close Control Drills

Number Seventy-Three - Drill: Cone Dribbling One Foot

A simple and handy drill we can practice easily on our own. Lay out ten cones no more than a meter apart to ensure that tight ball control is required. Using the inside and outside of the foot, knock the ball short distances to keep it close to the body. This is replicating running at an opponent prior to beating them.

Complete one run of the cones, then turn and return using the other foot. Complete ten double runs like this.

Key Skills:

- Close control,

- Using inside and outside of both feet,

- Working legs hard, by using short, fast steps.

Number Seventy-Four - Drill: Alternating Feet Dribble

We can then extend this drill by using both control the ball. With this we will run in a straighter line, but keep the ball close to feet. In a match situation we are tempting the defender to lunge in with a tackle, so that we can beat them with a piece of skill. To this end, try throwing in step overs and feints while dribbling.

Number Seventy-Five: Calf Workout with Dribble

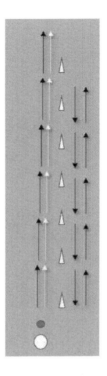

This drill fits neatly between ball control skills and warm up work. Set the cones about five meters apart. With smaller yards it might be necessary to put them into a square shape in order to have enough cones to make the drill worthwhile.

Dribble from cone one to cone two, keeping the ball under close control. At cone two, stop the ball dead, then back pedal back to cone one. Sprint onto the ball and dribble to cone three. Then back pedal once more to cone two. Repeat until the circuit is completed. We should aim to work at full speed in this drill to really give our calves a workout.

Number Seventy-Six: Juggle Dribbling

A fun exercise which is challenging but helps with balance and ball control. Place two cones 20 meters apart. We then juggle the ball while moving from one cone to another. We can set ourselves targets to improve this close control skill.

Target 1: No more than 2 drops of the ball between the cones.

Target 2: Get between the cones without dropping the ball,

Target 3: Start with a flick up to begin the Juggle dribbling,

Target 4: Include a turn at the end with the ball still juggling,

Target 5: Complete the maximum distance we can before the ball hits the ground.

Number Seventy-Seven - Drill: Random Dribbling

A handy drill which requires very little space. Place a number of cones randomly, but close together, say twelve cones in a space five meters by five meters. Using both feet, dribble around them, travelling as fast as we can. This will help us with changing direction while keeping the ball under close control.

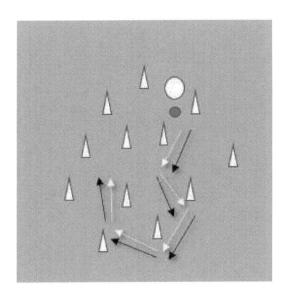

As we become better at the drill, we can develop it by adding in stops, where we stand on the ball, or turn quickly with a 360-degree rotation.

We will be working on the following key skills here:

- Close control,
- Moving and changing direction,
- Using both feet, and the inside and outside of the feet.

Number Seventy-Eight - Drill: Dribble and Sprint

This is a very true to life drill which helps us with dribbling with close control, then running with the ball at full speed to beat an opponent.

We place two sets of four cones one meter apart. There is a gap of fifteen meters between the two sets of cones.

With close dribbling, we navigate the first set of cones, sprint hard through the gap, propelling the ball with the laces, then complete close control once more. Turn, and repeat the drill in the opposite direction. Repeat ten times.

Key Skills:

- Close dribbling,
- Change of pace,
- Running with the ball,
- Turning.

Number Seventy-Nine - Drill: Dribble and ladders

This drill builds on the previous one, and combines multiple activities to develop calf muscles, pace and agility. Two balls, cones and a training ladder are needed.

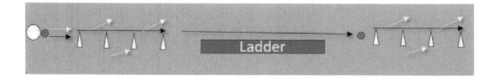

Set up as before but place the ladder in the gap. Start with one ball and place the other at the end of the ladder. Dribble through the cones and run with the ball to the ladder. Stop the ball and high step at full pace through the ladder. Collect the other ball and run to the cones. Navigate the cones with close dribbling skills, turn and repeat in the opposite direction.

Number Eighty - Drill: Equipment Free Close Control

This is a very difficult skill to master, but easy to set up. Place two cones at least 15 meters apart. Flick the ball up, juggling until it is under good control, then flick the ball high. Watch the ball carefully as it comes down and sweep the foot around to move the ball about three meters in the direct of the other cone. Sprint onto the ball, dribble to the cone and repeat.

The exercise can be developed by adding in a trick while dribbling between the cones, such as a step over or feint.

The key skills we are working on here are:

- Close control juggling,
- Watching the ball while turning the body on the half turn to receive it as it comes down,

- Sweeping the ball forwards, with the knee bent and head over the ball to keep it low,
- Cushioning the ball on contact so it does not move too far away on the touch,
- Running with the ball at speed.

Tip and Drill Number Eighty-One: High Level Close Control

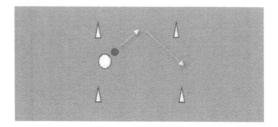

Make a square of cones so that we can run in various directions. Repeat drill eighty above, but experiment with ways of control the ball to improve dexterity.

Suggestions include:

- Controlling the ball on the top of the foot, toes up, so the ball is killed as it lands. (Perfect for the game situation where a long, high cross field ball is played, and the receiver is under partial pressure,
- Try stepping over the ball as it falls, and controlling with the back foot,

- Control with a juggle on the thigh,
- Control with the outside of the foot to instigate a rapid change of direction.

Number Eighty-Two - Drill: One player soccer tennis (very difficult)

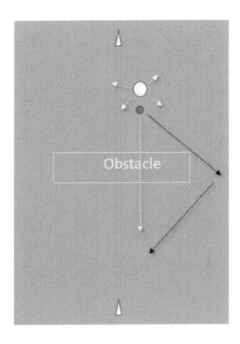

This is a very high-level drill. It is a really good one to suggest to a talented son or daughter who will enjoy working at it to perfect the skills involved.

Set up a pitch as follows: Two cones 12 meters apart. Between them an obstacle. Ideally this is something like a badminton net, or two poles with a tape between them, although a thin pop up goal could work.

The rules of the game are:

- Juggle the ball at least four times on one side of the central obstacle,
- Lob the ball over the obstacle so that it lands inside the far cone,
- One bounce allowed,
- Jog round the obstacle, and juggle at least four times on the other side,
- Repeat

Try to keep the game going as long as possible.

Number Eighty-Three - Tip: Exercising

Why not take a ball along on a daily walk or jog? Where lockdowns and social distancing allows such a trick, it is a simple to practice close dribbling control.

Mastering Technique

In this, our final chapter, we will offer simple guidance for the techniques of soccer. As we suggested earlier, we can use our camera phone to check our technique for whichever skill we are practicing is sound. We do not want to get into the habit of using poor technique, because that is very hard to break.

Where our technique is faltering, we can use the guidance below to correct the error.

Number Eighty-Four: Technique – Dribbling and Running with the ball

1) Use the laces to propel the ball,
2) Knock it two to five meters in front, depending on the space available in which to run,
3) Keep the head up,
4) Run at speed.

Number Eighty-Five: Technique – Three dribbling tricks

The Feint:

1) Dribble towards the opponent,

2) Approximately one meter away, plant one foot and drive off it to shift weight and direction the other way,

3) As this foot passes over the ball, drag it back in the opposite way to which we are heading, using the outside of the foot,

4) Kick off the other foot to change direction,

5) Accelerate into the space created.

The Step Over:

1) Dribble until approximately one meter from the opponent,

2) Turn the body in the direction you DO NOT intend to go, to fake the opponent,

3) Bring the foot you intend to use over and in front of the ball,

4) Touch it in the opposite direction with the outside of the foot,

5) Accelerate away.

6) Repeat steps 2-3 for the double step over but use the other foot.

The Nutmeg:

1) Dribble and slow when approximately one to two meters from the opponent,

2) Feint to get them to shift their weight, creating a gap between their legs,

3) Using the instep for accuracy, 'pass' the ball between their legs,

4) Sprint round them, on the opposite side to which they have lunged,

5) Accelerate away.

Number Eighty-Six: Technique – Turning

Cruyff Turn:

1) Using arms for balance, lean and swing the foot as though about to shoot or pass,
2) Use the instep to flick the ball back behind the non-kicking foot,
3) Change direction quickly,
4) Accelerate away
5) There are many turns we can use, practise ones of your own using the inside of the foot, the outside (hook turns), stepover turns and so forth.

Number Eighty-Seven: Technique – Shooting

1) Place the non-kicking foot beside the ball, 12 to 18 inches from it,
2) Keep our head down, and eyes on the ball,
3) Hit the ball in the middle,
4) Keep our weight over the ball to stop it rising over the bar,
5) Strike with the laces for power, with a smooth action and follow throw,
6) Ensure arms are out for balance.

Number Eighty-Eight: Technique – Passing inside and outside of the foot

Inside of foot:

1) Plant the non-kicking foot beside the ball,
2) Keep head still and arms out for balance,
3) Strike firmly through the ball using the instep,
4) Follow through,
5) A long instep pass will curve out then back in.

Outside of the foot:

1) Plant the non-kicking foot to the side and behind the ball,
2) Keep arms out for balance and head still,
3) Strike firmly across the ball with the outside of the boot,
4) The ball will curve away from where it is played, making it a perfect pass to use to play the ball inside a defender.

Number Eighty-Nine: Technique – Receiving the ball

1) Get on the half turn, this allows plenty of body between the ball and an opponent, and allow us to turn in either direction, or play a pass in either direction,
2) Keep arms out and slightly behind, to help sense the defense, and prevent a defender coming around to steal the ball,

3) Take the first touch to cushion the ball, sending it half a meter away from the foot,

4) Under pressure, this will normally be the outside of the front foot, although other control methods can be used,

5) Dribble, shoot or pass, turning if possible, playing backwards or laterally if tightly marked.

Number Ninety: Technique – Cushioning the Ball

1) Practice this if the ball is moving too far away from whichever part of the body is controlling it,

2) Give a little as the ball hits the part of the body, so it moves away, but not by far:

    a. For the foot, drop the foot back on contact, and bring our body weight over the ball,

    b. For other parts of the body, see below.

Number Ninety-One: Technique – Thigh Control

1) Extend the controlling thigh slightly forwards, with knee bent,

2) Ensure arms are out wide for balance and protection,

3) Get in line with the flight of the ball as early as possible,

4) Aim for the ball to hit midway between the knee and the top of the thigh,

5) Drop the thigh slightly on contact,

6) Quickly get into position to knock the ball forward with the foot as it hits the ground.

Number Ninety-Two: Technique – Chest Control

1) Get into position early, being in line with the flight of the ball,
2) Open the arms wide for balance, and to make the chest as large as possible,
3) On contact, drop the chest backwards so the ball drops,
4) Move it away from the body with the inside or outside of the foot.

Number Ninety-Three: Technique - Head Control

This is the hardest way to control a ball.

1) Get in line with the flight of the ball quickly,
2) While the ball is in flight, check quickly with the eyes to assess whether challenges will come in. Do not attempt to control a ball for which there will be a contest, instead flick it on or pass it back,
3) Open the arms wide for protection and balance,
4) Plant the feet firmly, bending the knees slightly,
5) Let the ball strike the middle of the forehead,
6) Angle the neck so the head is very slightly pointing up (to make the ball bounce up), and let the neck muscles give a fraction on contact to stop the ball bouncing away,

7) If necessary, add further controls with the chest or thigh before the ball lands in front of the feet.

Number Ninety-Four: Technique – Catching

1) Get in line with the ball quickly.

2) For a low ball,

    a. Have the fingers point down, and in,

    b. Cup the ball into the body, hugging it with the arms,

    c. For any shot below waist height, fall onto the ball, with the head over it, to stop it bouncing away.

3) For a high ball, above waist height,

    a. Have the arms ready, fingers pointing upwards,

    b. Spread the fingers,

    c. Catch with two hands behind the ball,

    d. If under no pressure, let the ball drop forwards, and catch it using the technique above. If under pressure, hold on, falling forwards if possible.

Number Ninety-Five: Technique – Dealing with Crosses

1) Make a quick decision whether we can reach the ball,

2) If so, decide whether to catch or punch,

3) If under pressure, either from opponents (or nearby teammates!) or because the ball is at the maximum of our stretch, we should punch,

4) If catching, use the technique described about, seeking to take the ball at the highest point possible (i.e. – at the apex of a leap and arms raised about the head),

5) If punching, leap for the ball, chest facing the direction of the cross,

6) Raise one knee in the leap for protection,

7) Extend the punching arm, thrusting it onto a closed fist,

8) Aim to hit the ball low, and on the side facing us, we are seeking height and distance on the punch

Conclusion – Keeping Mentally Fit

We hope that these drills and tips might help to give us some ideas of how we can practice at home during these difficult times. We are also confident that they provide interesting and creative ideas for soccer training at home at other times. We encourage our readers to vary the drills, adapting them to their own needs and interests.

However, we are also aware that there is an area of soccer fitness that we have unjustifiable neglected. We will look at this now. Physical fitness is very important to fulfilling our potential as a player, and so is technique. But we also need mental fitness. That is particular so during a time in which we might find ourselves isolated from friends and relatives.

Number Ninety-Six - Tip: Why Good Mental Health is Important Right Now

For many of us, life has suddenly and dramatically changed. The normal safety nets on which we rely are denied us. Soccer can help in three ways. Firstly, by working through the drills we have outlined in this book, we can stay physically in tune. Physical fitness is closely linked to mental well-being. It is well known that exercise releases happiness endorphins, and a soccer-based work out will give us a lift.

Secondly, it is a subject we can talk about on social media, and through online interaction with our friends and even with strangers. It is a global common link, and opens up conversations which will occupy our time, and make us feel busier and happier.

Thirdly, it is fun. Watching replays of old games, playing versions of online soccer games, playing some of the silly games listed as drills in this book, for example. Or building our own soccer resources.

On this point, we will finish our book with some non-physical soccer ideas we can use in the home. We will have a list of three of the best board games we can buy online; we will explain a very simple to play soccer patience game which can be played easily at home with a pack of cards, look at some at the best soccer based books we can read, and finally, list some of the best soccer based films we can find and watch.

Number Ninety-Seven - Tip: Best Soccer Based Games

Some of the following games are no longer produced, but all are freely available on sites such as Amazon, eBay and other online marketplaces.

Subbuteo: The king of soccer games. Small players with semicircular bases, felt pitch and goals with nets. All that is needed is a tabletop or floor space, an imagination and careful knees. (Note, if we kneel on a player, glue him back to his base. He will be shorter, with a lower center of gravity, and much easier to control!)

Chad Valley Soccer: If you can get one, a clever game with a shaped tin base. Could be an investment as well as a diversion.

Striker: Bash his head to score with superb chips. Any soccer fan of a certain age will remember this game.

Table Football/Fusball: A bit pricier, but well worth the investment. Keeps us fit as well as entertained.

Number Ninety-Eight - Tip: A Soccer Patience Card Game

Here's a time filling game that is easy to play. We invented it ourselves, so we are sure that players can improve it further.

Black Cards – Home Team

Red Cards – Away Team

Home teams have an advantage, so choose one red suit and remove the picture cards, reducing the scoring potential of the read team, and raising that of the black team.

How to Play:

- Shuffle the cards,

- Turn the cards over one at a time,
- The winning side is the one with the most goals scored, just like in soccer.
- Cards A-Jack relate to a player 1 to 11.
- If a player card, i.e. one of those above, and it is followed by a card of the same color a goal is scored if:
  - A Number 9 is followed by any card of the same color.
  - A Number 10 is followed by any card of the same suit.
  - Numbers 7, 8 and 11 are followed by a picture card or Ace of the same suit.
  - Numbers 4, 5, 6 are followed by a consecutive number of the same color.
  - Numbers 2 or 3 are followed by a consecutive number of the same suit.
- Handicaps can be added by taking more cards away at the beginning.

Run leagues, cup competitions, or just design our own game.

Number Ninety-Nine - Tip: Best Soccer Books

Fever Pitch: Nick Hornby's tale of young adulthood in London set against the background of the tough defensive Arsenal team of the late 1980s and early 1990s. Perhaps the greatest semi fictional soccer book of all time.

Puskas on Puskas – The Life and Times of a Footballing Legend: Ferenc Puskas. An autobiographical account of the life and career of one of the best players to ever step onto a field.

The Damned United: David Peace. The story of perhaps the world's most under rated manager, Brian Clough, who achieved miracles with second class teams, but somehow managed to rile anybody in authority.

Foul! The Secret World of FIFA: Bribes, Vote Rigging and Ticket Scandals: Andrew Jennings blows the cover off the appalling institution that was FIFA under Sepp Blatter.

AJ Rutherford's Russian World Cup in Russia: Alan Peter's comic look at the 2018 World Cup through the eyes of a self-proclaimed expert pundit, Aiden Rutherford. A man who would be better off watching his own domestic situation rather than boasting about his expert knowledge of world soccer. And does he really have an 'expert source' in every camp?

Number One Hundred: Two Yards Out, Open Goal and He Hits it Over…Soccer Films – worth a watch for comedy value.

Here we go. Sorry.

Bend it Like Beckham: This shouldn't really be on this list, because the culture clash film is really quite good.

Shaolin Soccer: This is more like it. A Shaolin disciple motivates his brothers and forms a soccer team in which martial arts play a major role. Presumably Diego Simeone is their manager.

The Arsenal Stadium Mystery: 1939. Most interesting for a pre-war look at London. Or for a chance to see the acting skills of genuine footballers such as Cliff Bastin and George Allison.

Goal, The Dream Begins: One reviewer says of this film, 'Goal is a very good soccer film'; well, somebody had to. Perhaps we should take note of the caveat, 'soccer' film. Made in cooperation with FIFA, which is not necessarily a selling point.

Escape to Victory: The Godfather of them all. Who really thought that an aging Michael Caine and the most unbelievable keeper ever, in Sylvester Stallone, could play football? Somebody did, which might explain why he also thought Pele could act.

Get in a few beers, you do not want to watch this sober. But, like being flattened by a flabby center half, and nutmegged by a fifteen-year-old half your age, watching Escape to Victory is a rite of passage every adult soccer fan must, we are sad to say, go through.

We do not know of any soccer film which has won an Oscar. There is a good reason for this. As a genre, it is not the one which lends itself to quality film making. Despite that, we can enjoy them often for their very badness.

And we can take heart, films like Escape to Victory will, at least, be over soon. So, to, thankfully, will the Corona Virus pandemic.

Stay fit, stay healthy, stay active, stay positive, stay safe.

Made in the USA
Monee, IL
13 September 2021